New Hands, New Life
Robots, Prostheses and Innovation

New Hands, New Life

Robots, Prostheses and Innovation

Alex Mihailidis
Jan Andrysek

FIREFLY BOOKS

A FIREFLY BOOK

Published by Firefly Books Ltd. 2017

First printing

Publisher Cataloging-in-Publication Data (U.S.)

Names: Mihailidis, Alex, author. | Andrysek, Jan, author.
Title: New Hands, New Life : Robots, Prostheses and Innovation / Alex Mihailidis, Jan Andrysek.
Description: Richmond Hill, Ontario, Canada : Firefly Books, 2017. | Includes index. | Summary: People with physical disabilities are experiencing new freedom through advances in science and technology.
Identifiers: ISBN 978-1-77085-969-2 (hardcover) 978-1-77085-991-3 (paperback)
Subjects: LCSH: Prosthesis – Juvenile literature. | Self-help devices for people with disabilities – Juvenile literature. | BISAC: JUVENILE NONFICTION / Health & Daily Living / Physical Impairments. | JUVENILE NONFICTION / Technology / Inventions.
Classification: LCC RD698.A537 | DDC 617.033 – dc23

Library and Archives Canada Cataloguing in Publication

Mihailidis, Alex, 1974-, author
    New hands, new life : robots, prostheses and innovation / Alex Mihailidis, Jan Andrysek.
Includes index.
ISBN 978-1-77085-969-2 (hardcover).--ISBN 978-1-77085-991-3 (softcover)
    1. People with disabilities--Juvenile literature. 2. Robots--Technological innovations--Juvenile literature. 3. Prosthesis--Technological innovations--Juvenile literature. I. Andrysek, Jan, author II. Title.
RD130.M54 2017   j617.9   C2017-901996-1

Published in the United States by
Firefly Books (U.S.) Inc.
P.O. Box 1338, Ellicott Station
Buffalo, New York 14205

Published in Canada by
Firefly Books Ltd.
50 Staples Avenue, Unit 1
Richmond Hill, Ontario L4B 0A7

Cover and interior design:
Gareth Lind, LINDdesign
Illustrations: Nick Craine
Printed in China

Canada We acknowledge the financial support of the Government of Canada.

Contents

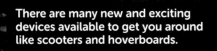

There are many new and exciting devices available to get you around like scooters and hoverboards.

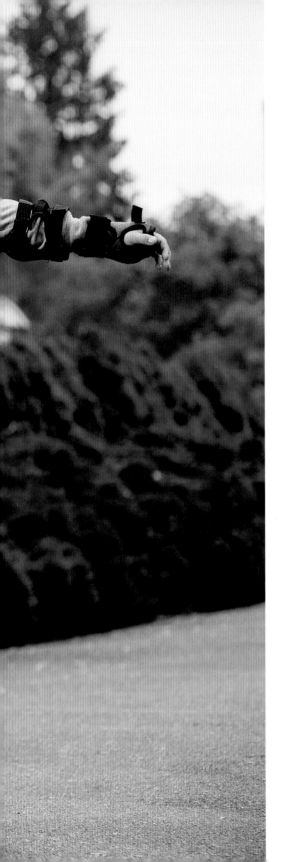

Introduction

Many of us use machines in our everyday lives. Cars and bikes take us places. Computers help us with schoolwork. Phones allow us to stay in touch with friends and family. But for people living with a major disability, machines are especially important. Assistive technologies allow a man with a missing leg to walk, a woman with a missing arm to hold objects, or a child in a wheelchair to play a sport. In this book, you will learn how our bodies allow us to do physical activities, and what happens when our bodies don't work properly. You will also learn how machines called assistive technologies can help. From artificial limbs and wheelchairs to exoskeletons and robots, amazing machines are making it possible for people with disabilities to lead healthy, active lives.

1 How We Move

Think about the things you do in a typical day. You get dressed, play with toys, go to school, take part in sports and eat meals. But have you ever stopped to think about how you are able to do these things? How do your legs know that you want to walk? How are you able to reach out, pick something up and hold it in your hands?

The answer lies in the amazing, complex machine that is your body. All day long, every single day, you use different parts of your body—your bones, your muscles and your brain—to help you move around and interact with the world.

Bone Basics

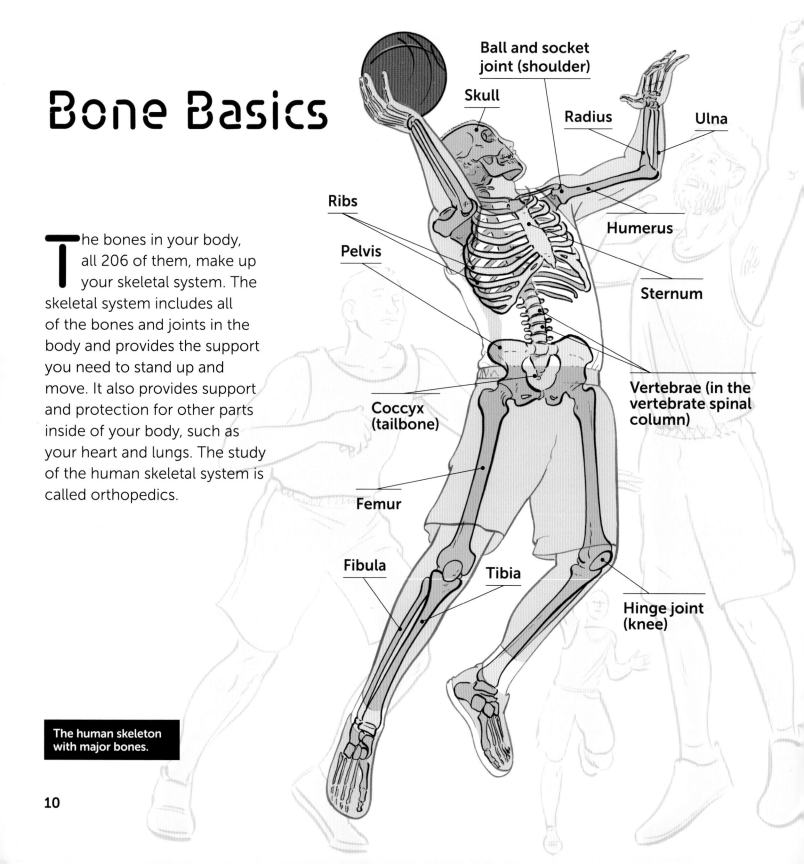

The bones in your body, all 206 of them, make up your skeletal system. The skeletal system includes all of the bones and joints in the body and provides the support you need to stand up and move. It also provides support and protection for other parts inside of your body, such as your heart and lungs. The study of the human skeletal system is called orthopedics.

Ball and socket joint (shoulder)

Skull

Radius

Ulna

Ribs

Humerus

Pelvis

Sternum

Vertebrae (in the vertebrate spinal column)

Coccyx (tailbone)

Femur

Fibula

Tibia

Hinge joint (knee)

The human skeleton with major bones.

Meet Your Bones

- The longest bone in the human body is the *femur*, or thigh bone.
- The smallest bone in the human body is the *stapes* (or stirrup) bone. It's found in the middle ear and is only 0.11 inches (2.8 mm) long.
- Broken bones will regrow and repair themselves. Doctors will often use a cast or splint to make sure broken bones heal straight.
- There are a number of skeletal disorders: arthritis is an inflammatory disease that damages joints; osteoporosis is a disease that increases the chance of fractures; and scoliosis is a curvature of the spine.

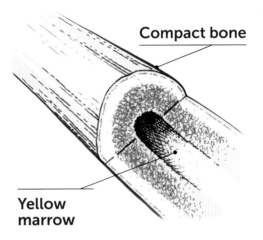

Compact bone

Yellow marrow

A cross-section of bone.

- Most human bones have a dense, strong outer layer, a spongy part full of air and a core of soft, flexible tissue called marrow.

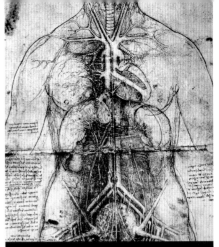

Leonardo da Vinci dissected human cadavers to learn how they worked. He made detailed notes and drawings of his findings.

The study of human anatomy—the examination of body parts such as bones, muscles and other organs—may be the oldest medical science. In the fifth century BCE, Greek scientists had developed theories about how the blood moved through the body. In the 11th century, the first university was established in Bologna, and by 1196, it included a medical school. In the 15th century, artist Leonardo da Vinci was dissecting human cadavers in order to learn more about what they were made of and how they worked. He made detailed notes and drawings of his findings. Since da Vinci's time, scientists have developed much more sophisticated tools to study the human body. Today, magnetic resonance imaging (MRI) devices allow us to view bones and muscles without having to open up the body.

An x-ray of a bone fracture of a child's forearm. Bones regrow and repair themselves.

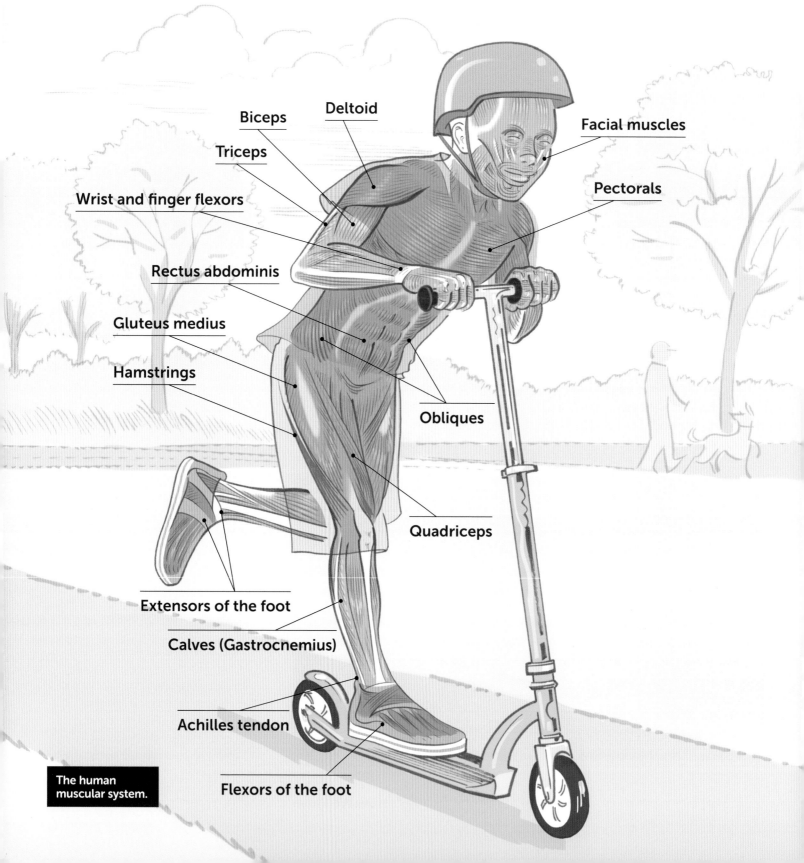

Biceps

Deltoid

Facial muscles

Triceps

Pectorals

Wrist and finger flexors

Rectus abdominis

Gluteus medius

Hamstrings

Obliques

Quadriceps

Extensors of the foot

Calves (Gastrocnemius)

Achilles tendon

Flexors of the foot

The human muscular system.

Muscle Mania

Sure, your bones hold you up, but they can't do much without muscles. There are more than 600 muscles in your body, and combined, they make up half of your weight. Muscles are tough, elastic structures connected to bones by cord-like tendons. Tendons allow your muscles to pull on your bones, which is how you are able to move. If you wiggle your fingers, you can see the tendons on the back of your hand move as they do their work. Together, your muscles, bones and joints make up your musculoskeletal system.

Meet Your Muscles

- The word muscle is derived from the Latin *musculus*, meaning "little mouse." This might be because of the shape of some muscles—or because when muscles contract under the skin they look like a little mouse moving under a rug.
- The *gluteus maximus*, which is located on your back side, is the largest muscle in the human body. It needs to be strong enough to allow you to stand up straight and walk.
- The tongue has eight muscles that help you to eat and swallow food.

- At just over 0.04 inches (1 mm) in length, the *stapedius* is the smallest skeletal muscle in the human body. It is located in the middle ear.
- The heart's cardiac muscle does the most work of any muscle over a lifetime.
- If all of the muscles in your body pulled in one direction at the same time, you could lift 25 tons, which is almost like lifting/pulling five elephants.

It takes 17 muscles to smile, and 43 to frown.

Brains on the Brain

Bones and muscles are important, but they need the brain to help them work. The brain and its network of nerves act like the body's central computer: they coordinate all the parts of the musculoskeletal system and make movement possible. There are many different parts of the brain that help you to do an amazing number of things. The brain controls how your body works. It controls how quickly your heart pumps blood and the pace of your breathing. It controls your physical movement when walking, talking, standing and sitting. And your brain lets you think, make decisions and feel happy, sad or angry.

Meet Your Brain

- The human brain is more than three times as big as the brain of a similarly sized mammal.
- The brain is protected by the skull (or cranium), which consists of 22 bones joined together.
- An adult human's brain weighs about 3 pounds (1.4 kg). Although it makes up only 2 percent of the body's weight, it uses around 20 percent of its energy.

- Diseases of the brain include Alzheimer's, Parkinson's and multiple sclerosis, all of which limit the normal function of the brain.
- Traumatic brain injury (TBI) occurs when the brain is injured by extreme movements and impacts to the head. In severe cases, the brain injury may affect a person's ability to properly control bodily movements. TBIs can usually be prevented by wearing helmets for activities such as bicycling or skiing.

A human brain with nerves.

Motor control is the process by which humans and animals use their brain/cognition to activate and coordinate the muscles and limbs involved in the performance of a motor skill.

The movements your muscles make are controlled by the brain—specifically, an area called the motor cortex. When you decide to move, the motor cortex sends an electrical signal through your spinal cord and nerves to your muscles, causing them to contract. It's this muscle contraction that makes your joints and bones move. The motor cortex on the right side of your brain controls the muscles on the left side of your body, and the motor cortex on the left side of the brain controls the muscles on the right side of your body.

2 When Things Go Wrong

When your bones, muscles and brain are all working as they should, you can do pretty much anything. But what happens when something goes wrong? There are many different conditions that can cause a body not to operate as it is supposed to. Some of these conditions are caused by illness or disease, while others  occur due to an injury. Some happen before a person is born, while others might occur as a person ages. Some older people have problems walking and moving around because their bodies are not working as well as they did when they were younger.

Diseases

There are many different types of walkers that can help people of all ages to move around and be more independent.

Different diseases can affect the body in different ways. Some affect muscles, making them weaker than they should be. Others affect the brain and its ability to send signals to the rest of the body. Either way, the result can be difficulty in moving one's body.

Cerebral Palsy

Cerebral palsy (CP) is caused by brain damage that occurs before or during birth, or early in childhood. CP affects the muscles' ability to move the body in a normal way. Many children with CP not only have difficulty walking, but also experience speech problems and learning disabilities.

Stroke

A stroke occurs when there is poor blood flow to the brain, resulting in part of the brain not functioning properly. A stroke can happen when people have medical problems such as high blood pressure. While many people recover after suffering a stroke, others may have permanent problems with parts of their bodies not working as they should. They may not be able to walk or talk properly.

Cancer

Your body—including your muscles and bones—is made up of millions of tiny structures called cells. Cancer is a disease that affects the cells, causing them to grow non-stop and out of control. Sometimes cancer can affect the bones in a person's arm or leg. When the cancer affects a large part of the bone, the entire limb must be removed. This is called an amputation.

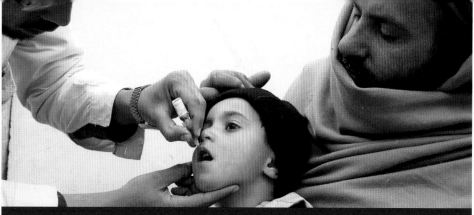

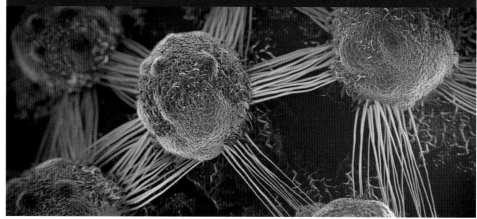

Above: Health worker administers polio-vaccine drops to a child in Pakistan.
Below: Illustration of cancer cells.

Spina Bifida

Spina bifida is caused when the spine does not form properly as the fetus grows in the mother's womb. A child born with spina bifida is likely to have difficulty walking as they grow up. They may also face challenges in their ability to learn. The severity of spina bifida can vary greatly, resulting in children having different disabilities or abilities.

Polio

Polio, or poliomyelitis, is a disease caused by an infection. For a small number of people, polio can result in permanent weakness of the muscles in the legs and in other parts of the body. Thanks to a vaccine, polio is no longer a problem in many places around the world. Over the past 25 years, the number of people affected by polio has dropped from more than 300,000 to less than 100. All of the present cases are outside of North America.

Crutches and not a prosthesis sometimes makes for the best soccer playing.

Injuries and Paralysis

Tennis player Jordanne Whiley of Great Britain in action during Wheelchair Quad Singles semifinal match at US Open 2015.

Spinal Cord Injury

When your spinal cord is injured, the brain is no longer able to send the signals needed to tell your muscles to move. And when a person loses the ability to move their muscles, the result is paralysis. Paralysis of the muscles, arm and leg on one side of the body is called hemiplegia. Paralysis of both legs is called paraplegia, and paralysis of both arms and both legs is called quadriplegia. Paralysis may be temporary or permanent, depending on the disease or injury.

Amputations

Very severe accidents or diseases can result in the loss of an arm or leg, which is called an amputation. An amputation is performed by a doctor after a severe injury, an infection, or a disease makes it impossible to save the limb. An amputation can occur as the result of traumatic events, such as car crashes, or from accidents involving lawnmowers and farm equipment. Common amputations include a finger, foot or leg.

WW1 era uniformed U.S. soldier with both of his legs amputated. Ca. 1918–19.

Helping People with Amputations

There are several organizations throughout North America that help people with amputations. In the United States, the Amputee Coalition is dedicated to enhancing the quality of life for amputees and their families, improving patient care and preventing limb loss. In Canada, The War Amps was established in 1918 to help wounded war veterans returning home from the First World War. Today, they offer financial support and help children with amputations meet with and learn from others about how to better deal with their challenges.

Machines That Help

Around the world, nearly 15 percent of people live with a disability. That's over a billion people, including about 100 million children. Two hundred million people have disabilities severe enough that they might not be able to walk, or do everyday things such as feeding themselves.

About 10 million people around the world have a major amputation, and 6 million people live with severe paralysis in North America alone.

Whether a person is paralyzed or is missing a limb due to an amputation, different types of machines can help to restore some function. Some commonly used machines called assistive technologies include prostheses (artificial limbs), orthoses (braces) and wheelchairs. Assistive technologies allow people with disabilities to do almost anything. With an assistive device, a person can get around, walk, run, work, play sports and participate in other recreational activities.

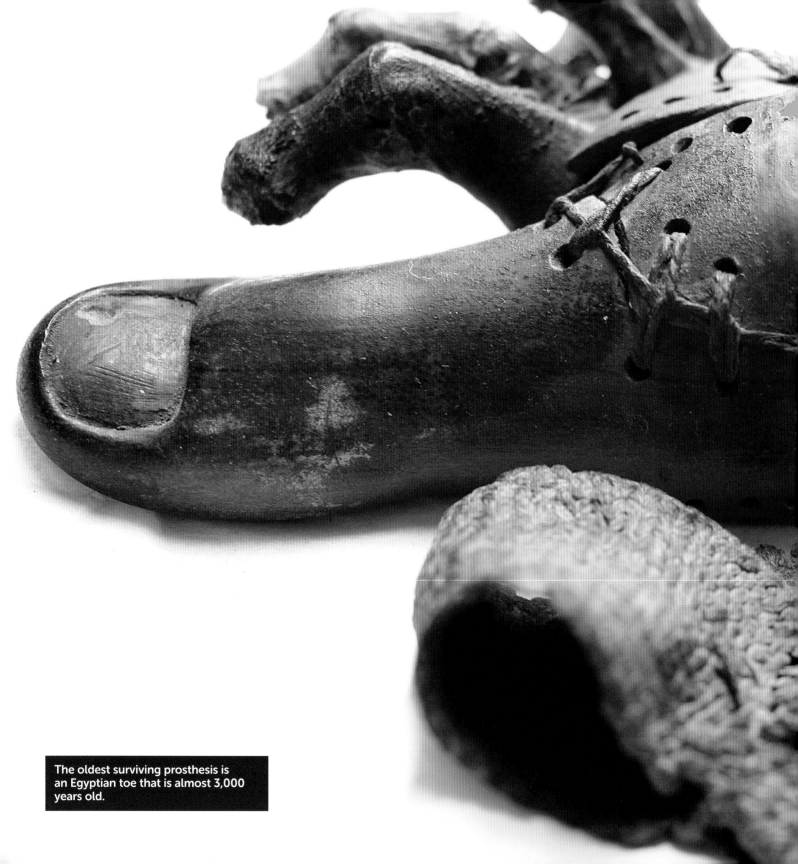

The oldest surviving prosthesis is an Egyptian toe that is almost 3,000 years old.

History of Assistive Technologies

People have been developing assistive technologies for longer than you might think.

Mummy Toes?

Recently, a prosthetic toe belonging to a mummy was found, making it the oldest prosthesis ever discovered. Another old prosthetic leg was made from bronze, iron and wood. It was likely quite heavy compared to modern prostheses, which are made of strong and light metals and plastics. These days, hydraulics provide smooth movements, and computers and motors control the movements. Prostheses are getting smarter and better all the time, making them easier to use.

From Sticks to Orthoses

No one really knows who developed the first orthosis, or brace, but it was likely a long time ago, and may have come from the need to support a broken arm or leg. Originally, people likely just tied some sticks to the broken part of the body. Orthoses have come a long way since then!

The Invalid's Chair?

In 1595, Phillip II of Spain needed help getting around. An inventor created the first wheelchair, called an "invalid's chair." Things have changed a lot since then. Push wheels came first, and then, in 1916, motors. By 1932, a folding version was available. Specialized wheelchairs are now available for specific activities, such as tennis or basketball. Mind-controlled models are also on the market.

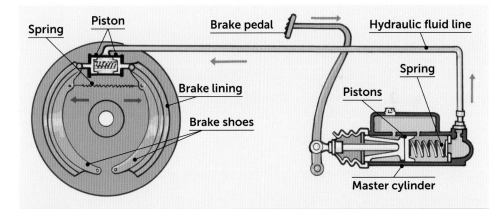

Hydraulics Help

Hydraulics are pretty common in everyday life. The brakes in your family car run on hydraulics. When the brake pedal is pressed, the action pushes a liquid, such as oil, which applies force on the brakes at the wheels. Because hydraulic systems produce a lot of pressure and force in a small amount of space, a hydraulic-controlled prosthesis doesn't get too heavy and bulky. Hydraulic systems also create smooth movements.

As part of the Agility Clinic held at the Holland Bloorview Kids Rehabilitation Hospital in Toronto, Canada, children with limb amputations are encouraged to participate in physical activities alongside their non-amputee peers, realizing their many abilities.

All About Prostheses

A prosthesis is a replacement for a part of the body that is missing. Sometimes prosthetic limbs are called artificial limbs. Prostheses can be used to improve a person's appearance or to replace an important function that has been lost. Some prostheses can do both. A prosthetic eyeball, for example, is used only to improve someone's appearance (since no sight is possible). A prosthetic leg, though, allows a person to walk while also making the leg appear complete.

Types of Prostheses

A prosthesis is usually named after the part of the body it replaces. Lower-limb prostheses refer to the legs, while upper-limb prostheses refer to the arms. A person can have a prosthetic finger or toe, or a full arm or leg. Arm and leg prostheses are much more complicated and difficult to build.

Prosthetics Enable Great Things

When she was 22 years old, Daniela Garcia lost parts of both her arms and legs in a train accident. Now, she uses four prostheses. Using her prostheses, Daniela has accomplished more than many people. She works as a doctor to help others, has written a book and is now the mother of two young boys. She is an inspiration to many learning to live without the use of their legs and arms.

Model Rebekah Marine poses for a photo with her prosthetic hand at a designer fitting and casting event at King's College in New York City.

These children use their upper limb protheses for gripping.

Upper-Limb Prostheses

There are two common types of upper-limb prostheses.

Body-Powered Prostheses

A body-powered prosthesis is a purely mechanical device, with movements powered by other parts of the person's body. With this type of prosthesis, cables are commonly used to transfer movement from one part of the body to the prosthesis. For example, a person may use their shoulder to pull on a cable that opens or closes a prosthetic hand.

Myoelectric Prostheses

A myoelectric prosthesis taps into the electrical activity of the body's muscles, specifically in the remaining part of the arm. These electrical signals are tiny, and special sensors are needed to detect them. Electronics are then used to make the signals stronger so that they can be used by computers built into the hand. The computers determine how to move the arm, or whether to open or close the hand, and send the appropriate signal to motors in the prosthesis. Myoelectric devices are more complex than body-powered prostheses, but they can provide better functionality.

Advanced Arm Prostheses

Prosthetic limbs are becoming more and more sophisticated. For example, modern prosthetic hands can have fingers that move individually to provide different types of grasps, and hold different types of objects—one grasp might be used to hold a pen, while a different grasp is needed to grip a hammer or carry luggage. This makes it possible for the prosthesis to function more like a biological body part and to do a greater variety of things.

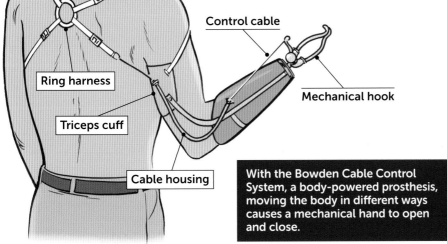

Control cable

Mechanical hook

Ring harness

Triceps cuff

Cable housing

With the Bowden Cable Control System, a body-powered prosthesis, moving the body in different ways causes a mechanical hand to open and close.

These individuals are all using the All-Terrain knee joint, first when it was a prototype in its early stage of research and development (left) and now as a product that is sold and used around the world (right) by a Canadian social enterprise called LegWorks.

Lower-Limb Prostheses

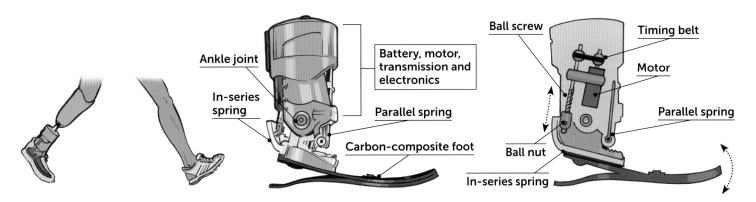

Ankle joint

In-series spring

Battery, motor, transmission and electronics

Parallel spring

Carbon-composite foot

Ball screw

Timing belt

Motor

Parallel spring

Ball nut

In-series spring

ower-limb prostheses can include parts such as a foot, ankle joint, knee joint and hip joint, depending on what is required. The entire prosthesis attaches to the body using a socket. An artificial leg needs to be strong, since it must carry a person's weight—and may take millions of steps every year! The socket also needs to be extra comfortable, much like a shoe if you are going on a long hike.

Passive Prostheses

Most prosthetic legs are passive. This means they do not move on their own. Instead, the person must learn to use the muscles in the rest of their body to control and move the prosthesis. For example, a person with a leg prosthesis can use hip muscles to control the movement and bending of the prosthetic knee. To help with this, most prosthetic legs also have special braking or locking mechanisms to prevent the leg from bending at the knee. This helps to avoid falls. Prosthetic legs may also have damping mechanisms to help make movements smooth so the person does not get tired too easily.

Advanced Leg Prostheses

Modern prosthetic legs use various electronics and on-board computers to better control the prosthesis. The leg can automatically adjust its movements to allow a person to walk better and more efficiently. Prosthetic researchers and engineers are trying hard to make leg prostheses capable of moving on their own, as if they had built-in muscles. They have already developed powered knees and ankles, which use motors to act like muscles, and allow amputees to more easily walk up stairs, stand up and push off when walking.

Specialized Prostheses and Assistive Technologies

These days, there are many prosthetic technologies designed for specific activities: aerobics and gymnastics, baseball, bowling, canoeing, kayaking, bike riding, dancing, drumming, golf, guitar playing, hockey, horseback riding, lacrosse, monkey bars, photography, pool playing, racket sports, rock climbing, skipping and violin playing— to name just a few. If you've ever watched the Paralympics, you may have seen a few of these specialized prostheses in action.

Former Zambezi river guide Paul Templer, who lost his left arm in a hippopotamus attack in 1996, paddles a kayak with a specially made paddle. Templer canoed the entire 1,600-mile length of the Zambezi River in 1998 to raise funds for a prosthetics factory to aid land mine victims in Mozambique and Angola.

Physicist Stephen Hawking sits on stage during an announcement of the Breakthrough Starshot initiative where he spoke through his voice synthesizer.

Technologies for Speech, Hearing and Sight

For those unable to talk, advances made in electronic speech synthesis can help those without a voice express themselves verbally. A computer and speech synthesizer is used by English theoretical physicist Stephen Hawking. Although current computers are very capable of pronouncing words, they find word emphasis difficult. However, Hawking's computer-generated voice has become recognized worldwide as uniquely his own.

A former client at Holland Bloorview Kids Rehabilitation Hospital in Toronto, Adrian Anantawan was able to play violin with an adaptive device known as a "spatula." Here he plays violin at a reception announcing the Global Cultural Initiative in the East Room of the White House.

Technology can allow deaf individuals to hear. This hearing device, known as a cochlear implant, works by picking up sound from a microphone around the ear and transmitting it to the part of the brain that processes sound.

Researchers are working on ways to restore sight to the blind. Experiments with electronic eyes utilize small cameras near the eye to capture images and send signals to the optic nerves, which are in turn sent to the brain.

Prostheses for Everyone

An orthopedic clinician learns to use a 3D scanning app to capture data for a child's 3D-printed ankle-foot orthosis using an iPad Mini.

Making Less Expensive Prostheses

Researchers, engineers and prosthetists are continually coming up with new ways of making prosthetic legs and arms—ways that are easier, faster and cheaper. All three are important when it comes to making sure that people who need a new arm or leg can get one, especially when you consider that more than one prosthesis may be needed over the course of a person's life. As a child grows, for example, the prosthesis needs to grow with them. Some children may need up to 25 different prostheses in their lifetime, while some adults will need between 15 and 20.

The Niagara Foot and the All-Terrain Knee

Researchers in the United States and Canada are trying to design prosthetic feet and knees that work well but cost little to make. They're doing this by using

Prostheses can be very expensive, often costing more than a car, and many people cannot afford them. As a result, many cannot go to school or work for a living. Thankfully, people all around the world are trying to help by developing prostheses that work well but are not as expensive. How about using a bicycle seat as a prosthetic foot? Or plumbing pipes to make a socket and leg?

innovative mechanical designs and more economical manufacturing processes. For example, the Niagara Foot—which was made in Canada and is now in use around the world—is designed to provide smoothness and springiness just like much more expensive prosthetic feet. The AT-Knee (All-Terrain Knee) was also developed by researchers in Canada. It makes it possible for people to walk on rough terrain safely and efficiently, and it is being used in many developing countries as well as throughout North America and Europe.

Eight-year-old Pisith tries out his first 3D-printed ankle-foot orthosis (LHS).

Four-year-old Roseline was the first person to be fitted with a 3D-printed below-the-knee prosthetic socket as part of a clinical study.

More Help Needed

According to the World Health Organization, only 5 to 15 percent of the people who need mobility technologies have access to them. Prosthetic limbs provide greater mobility and independence, but wooden crutches are the only mobility device available to some children with lower-limb disabilities.

A 3D printer produces prosthetic hands.

A Whole New Dimension

New technologies such as 3D printers are cutting down the costs of making prostheses by simplifying the process. The first step is to scan the residual limb—the part of the body where the prosthesis will be attached—to understand its shape and to make the new prosthesis fit properly and comfortably. This results in a very detailed image of the body part. Next, this image is edited and turned into a precise model of the artificial limb. Finally, the completed model is used to print the prosthetic device. Once printed, the prosthetic device can be further modified by a technician using simple tools to make sure that it fits properly.

A special brace can provide stability to children who pronate. Children with low muscle tone or who have trouble with stability can walk, run and jump with the help of a brace.

Orthoses

An orthosis is a type of brace that helps to support or move a part of the body. There are orthoses for the upper limbs (hands and arms), lower limbs (legs) and spine. How do they work? Imagine a person who has been paralyzed from a stroke. They might not be able to control their leg muscles or support themselves. If they tried to stand, their leg might bend and they could fall. An orthosis can help support the leg and prevent it from bending, so that the person can safely stand and even walk.

Light and Easy

An orthosis must be specially built by an orthotist, so that it comfortably surrounds the body and provides support. Orthoses used to be made mostly from leather and metals. The leather part of an orthosis allowed it to be comfortably worn throughout the day, much like a leather shoe. The metal parts provided the support. More modern orthoses are made from plastics instead of leather and lighter, stronger metals. This makes them lighter, easier to clean, easier to put on and take off and more comfortable to use.

Advanced Orthoses

While most orthoses are just supports, some more sophisticated types are designed to allow movement. For example, a long leg brace can have a mechanism that locks the knee joint when a person with weak leg muscles puts their weight on the braced leg, and unlocks the knee when weight is removed. This makes it possible for the person to safely walk while still having a leg that bends naturally at the knee.

An orthosis supports a part of the body that does not function the way it should. Specially made devices can be worn throughout the day and at home, enabling individuals to walk and move.

Wheelchairs

Some people with paralysis or other diseases use wheelchairs to get around and stay active. A wheelchair can be efficient and easy to use, especially over long distances, so some people may choose to use both a wheelchair and a prosthesis or orthosis, depending on where they need to go. Although wheelchairs do have some limitations—they can't go up and down stairs, for example, and can be difficult to manage in tight spaces—they do play a very important role in helping people get around.

Over the years, wheelchairs have become more advanced. The most important change may be the development of lighter materials, like titanium. Named after the Greek god Titan—known for his enormous strength—titanium chairs are much easier to manage than older varieties.

Manual Wheelchairs

Like body-powered prostheses, some wheelchairs require body power to work. The person using the wheelchair can move themselves by grabbing the top of the wheels and pushing forward. Help can also be provided by having someone else push from behind.

Powered Wheelchairs

Some wheelchairs use electric motors to move. A joystick is used to make the wheelchair go faster, slow down and turn left and right. For people who cannot use their arms to control a joystick—for example, a person who is paralyzed in both the upper and lower limbs—innovative ways to control the wheelchair have been developed. One common way is a "Sip and Puff" control, which uses a tube into which the person blows and sips. Electronics built into the chair help with the movement. For example, a strong puff may move the chair forward, while a soft sip may make the wheelchair go left.

Advanced Wheelchairs

While many wheelchairs are designed simply to help people get around, others can do amazing things. Some are built to travel well over very rough ground, like in the woods or on a hiking trail. Some allow a person to race in marathons and sprints, play sports like rugby or basketball, and even climb stairs. And some have special seats that allow a person to be in different positions—from sitting upright to lying perfectly flat. Some even have a seat that can help a person to stand up so they can be on the same level as someone who is not in a wheelchair.

4 Working Together

Assistive technologies such as prostheses, orthoses and wheelchairs can greatly help people with disabilities. But it is important to remember that they are only tools. Before anyone can benefit from these assistive technologies, they must first heal and recover. The assistive device must then be properly made and the person must be trained on how best to use it.

Prosthetists specialize in fitting and making limbs and other assistive technologies.

A small child being fitted by her prosthetist and therapist with her first prosthetic hand.

A Perfect Fit

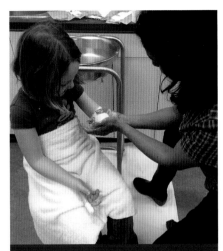

A mold is made to ensure that the prosthetic socket fits as comfortably as possible on the affected limb.

Most assistive technologies—including prostheses, orthoses and even the seats on wheelchairs—need to fit properly in order to be comfortable and work well. To make sure this happens, these technologies are built by professionals called prosthetists, orthotists and rehabilitation technicians. They must understand the clinical condition of the person for whom they are building, and then figure out what type of assistive device would work best. This is not always an easy job, given the many different types of injuries and the ways in which people want to use their technologies.

Comfort Is Key

For a prosthetic or orthotic device to work well, it must fit properly and attach to the body in the right way. Arms and legs are attached to your body by bones, joints, muscles, tendons and ligaments. An artificial limb or an orthotic brace must attach in a different way, but it still needs to act as part of the body. And it must be comfortable. Have you ever had a pair of uncomfortable shoes? You probably didn't want to walk too far in them, did you? A person using an assistive device would feel the same way about a poorly fitted artificial limb or brace, or a wheelchair seat that rubbed in the wrong places.

Making Molds

Prosthetists and orthotists have the expertise needed to make limbs and braces fit well. One way they do this is by paying close attention to the injured limb at the point where the prosthesis or brace will attach. In the case of a prosthesis, this attachment is called a prosthetic socket. Often, plaster bandages—like the ones used to create casts for healing broken arms or legs—are used to capture the shape. This shape can then be made into a mold to make the plastic socket or brace. These days, as we've seen, 3D imaging and printers are also being used to help get the best fit possible.

A person with a new prosthesis learns to walk holding onto parallel bars for support.

Practice, Practice, Practice

Once a person has been fitted with an assistive device, the next step is learning how to use it—and this can be hard work!

Learning to Walk

Those with lower-limb assistive technologies must learn to stand and balance before even thinking about learning to walk. Rehabilitation professionals such as prosthetists and therapists can help by suggesting various exercises and activities. And sometimes, robots help! In some cases, a machine such as the Lokomat—a robotic device into which a person is strapped—can move paralyzed legs until they learn to move again on their own.

Grasping and Moving

Individuals with upper-limb assistive technologies must learn to grasp and move objects. For example, a person with a myoelectric prosthesis must learn to move certain muscles in order to open or close the prosthetic hand or move their elbow or shoulder joint. And they need to practice everyday tasks—like gripping a bottle of water, moving it close to the mouth and tilting it to take a drink. With enough practice, it's possible to use a prosthesis to do the many things that we would normally do with our hands, arms and legs.

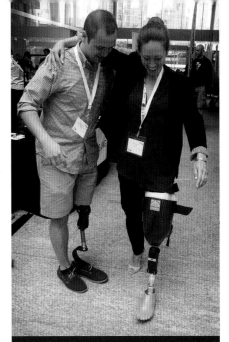

Brandon Burke helps another person try out the All-Terrain Knee for the first time.

Brandon Burke: Inspiring Others

Brandon Burke was an active young person who loved football, snowboarding and surfing. His life drastically changed as a teenager when he was diagnosed with cancer in his leg, which ultimately had to be amputated. After a long recovery, Brandon now uses a leg prosthesis to run, snowboard and stay active. He inspires many young amputees by showing them what is possible. He also works extremely hard to bring prostheses to the many people around the world who cannot afford them.

5 Putting Robots to Work

As new discoveries are made in the world of technology, important new inventions are being used to help kids and adults who need assistive technologies lead full and active lives. One such technology is robots. Whether they are at work in a lab, serving as an exoskeleton or providing artificial intelligence, robots are helping out.

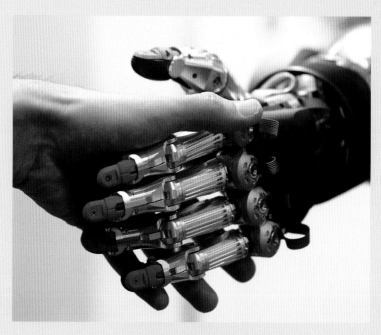

U.S. President Barack Obama shakes hands with a robotic arm operated by Nathan Copeland, a quadriplegic brain implant patient who can experience the sensation of touch and control a remote robotic arm with his brain, during a tour of the innovation projects at the White House Frontiers Conference.

A robot welds an automotive part in a car factory.

What Is a Robot?

Robots are all around us. We see them on television and in movies, but they are active in real life, too. Robots are often used to complete activities that are too dangerous for us to do on our own (certain types of mining or outer space exploration, for example) or for tasks that can be done more efficiently by a machine, like on factory assembly lines. These days, robots are also being used to support active and healthy lives.

Robot Basics

A robot is a machine that is meant to perform a specific task with great precision and accuracy. While there are many different types of robots, they all share certain characteristics that allow them to operate. All robots include:

• **Sensors:** A robot needs to understand what is happening in its surroundings, whether this is inside a factory, underwater or on a human body.

• **Movement:** A robot needs to be able to move and perform a task. Some robots move around on wheels or legs. Other robots—like the Canadarm or a child's prosthetic arm—have one or two moving parts.

• **Energy:** A robot needs power to operate. This power could come from a number of sources, including batteries, an electrical outlet or even energy sources like solar power.

• **Intelligence:** A robot needs to use the information from its sensors and other components to complete the task it's programmed to do. Humans take care of the programming, telling the robot what it should be doing and how to react to its environment.

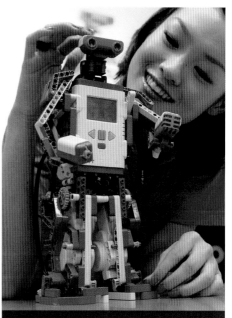

Build-it-yourself robot kits for home and school are available. They can be programmed in different ways and assembled in many configurations. The LEGO MINDSTORMS kit pictured is equipped with a 32-bit microprocessor, USB 2.0 and Bluetooth. Some can be fitted with cameras.

Robots called exoskeletons are worn on a person's arm or leg to help them regain use of their limb.

Robots and Prostheses

Robots are being used more and more to help people with disabilities, especially to design better and more intelligent assistive technologies, such as prostheses. For example, sensors can add the sensation of touch to a prosthetic hand. More recently, robotic limbs are now able to take signals from the human brain and translate them into motion.

Controlling Robotic Prostheses

In many ways, robotic prosthetic limbs are the same as any other robot. The big difference is that their components must work with the human body. These amazing technologies use biosensors to detect signals from the central nervous and muscular systems. Biosensors come in many different forms: surface electrodes detect electrical activity on the skin; needle electrodes are implanted directly into the muscle; and more advanced electrode arrays are embedded within the nerves themselves or inside the brain. Robotic prosthetic limbs can also use other types of sensors to understand things such as whether the hand at the end of the limb is opened or closed, or whether it is holding some kind of object.

Information from all of these different types of sensors travels to the controller or computer inside of the device, which acts like the "brain" of the robotic limb. The controller is connected to the robotic device and to the nervous and muscular systems. It takes signals and translates them into commands that are sent to the robotic device and its various components, such as a mechanical hand. The controller also interprets feedback from the various sensors on the device and sends that back to the brain.

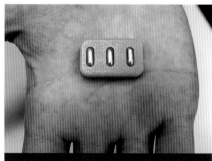

A myoelectric sensor can be fitted into a prothesis to detect electrical activity on the skin.

Myoelectric describes the electrical properties of muscles. A prosthetic that is myoelectrically controlled works with the electrical signals generated by the muscles. When particular muscles are intentionally flexed, special sensors relay information to the controller on the prosthesis, which translates the data into commands for the electric motors. The strength and speed of the movements in limbs and joints can be controlled by varying how much the muscle is flexed.

Mind Control

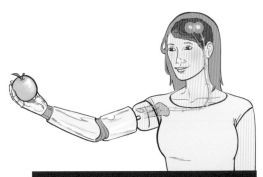

A bidirectional interface implant can be used to send signals both from the brain to the prosthetic arm and back again.

The controllers used by robotic limbs are becoming more and more advanced very quickly. Today they use artificial intelligence, which allows the technologies to act and respond like a real arm or leg. A key part of these new controllers is the ability to collect more sophisticated information about what the device should be doing directly from the brain. These new robotic limbs are known as mind-controlled (or thought-controlled) technologies.

Brain Work

Mind-controlled prostheses use different types of biosensors—called electrodes—that connect directly to the brain. Electrodes are inserted into the motor cortex. There, they measure the required signals from the brain, lighting up a circuit board in response to specific movements. The robotic limb is then programmed to move based on which part of the brain is "lighting up."

The number of electrodes required depends on how many movements are needed. In the case of a robotic arm, for example, opening and closing the hand is a relatively simple motion. But if a person needs to control all of the movements of his fingers, hundreds of electrodes might be required.

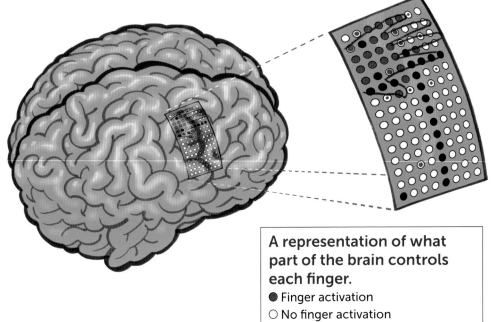

A representation of what part of the brain controls each finger.

- ● Finger activation
- ○ No finger activation
- ● Not available

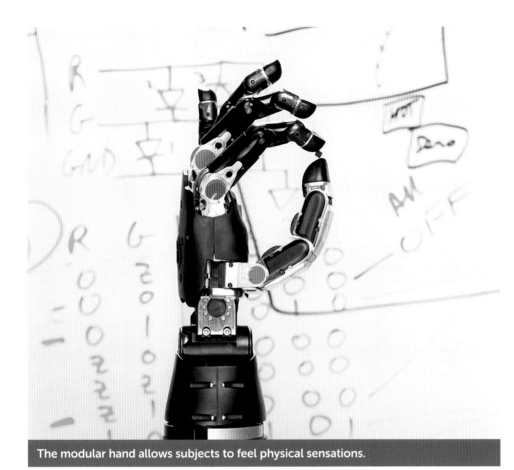

The modular hand allows subjects to feel physical sensations.

All kinds of new robots that can interact with people are being built.

Feel This!

The latest robotic limbs can even let a person "feel" an object that they are touching or holding. This is done with—you guessed it—more sensors! Pressure sensors, which are able to detect when pressure is being applied to them, are installed on the device, such as at the end of each finger on a robotic hand. When something pushes on these sensors, they convert that force into an electrical signal. These signals are transmitted to the brain through electrodes inserted into the sensory cortex, which helps us make sense of the information gathered by our five senses: vision, sound, smell, taste and touch. The sensory cortex uses the signals from the electrodes to "feel" the object being held.

Artificial Intelligence

The difference between people and computers is that people can make intelligent decisions based on past experiences. Maybe you've learned that you need to wait for a couple of minutes before eating your oatmeal. You know this because you've burned your mouth over and over again! Experiences like this can be thought of as "data" you've collected and stored in your brain. Turns out we can program computers to act in the same way. A computer can be programmed to collect data, recall data and make an intelligent decision based on what it has experienced in the past.

Exoskeletons

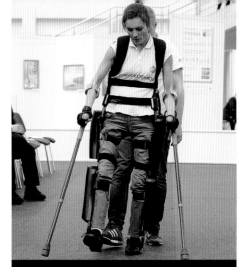

Exoskeletons that are worn on the legs are helping people who have lost the use of their legs to walk again.

What if a person still has their arm or leg, but can't use it anymore? Maybe paralysis has set in or strength has been lost due to aging or illness. Robots can help out here, too.

The Hardiman

Robots are being used to develop new technologies known as powered exoskeletons. These robotic machines can be worn on affected legs or arms to allow movement and enhance strength. Like any other robot, an exoskeleton has sensors, motors, levers and controllers that understand the kind of movements a person wants to make and helps them to do so as naturally as possible.

Exoskeletons weren't always so high-tech. The first real exoskeleton was codeveloped by General Electric and the United States military in the 1960s. The suit was named Hardiman, and it made lifting 250 pounds feel like lifting only 10 pounds. However, the Hardiman suit weighed almost 1,500 pounds (which is the same as a fully grown cow!). This made it impossible for people to use the Hardiman in everyday activities.

The Hardiman, the first exoskeleton.

Power Up!

Exoskeletons have come a long way since the Hardiman. Today's models feature braces and linkages that are strapped to the legs, hips and waist. The linkages are powered by precisely positioned motors that help a person walk. Exoskeletons also use sensors to know when a person is trying to move. This allows the linkages to position themselves correctly to make the person's walking motion as natural as possible. These exoskeletons use a small computer that is typically worn as a backpack or around the waist. This computer gives the device "intelligence," allowing it to operate in different environments and on different surfaces, including going up and down stairs. The pack also holds a battery so the device can operate for a day before recharging.

Robots that are worn on the upper body can help people regain use of their arms and legs and to do activities that they normally couldn't have without them.

Help for the Upper Half

Exoskeletons can also help our shoulders, arms, hands and even fingers. Upper body work is often hard work! Construction workers pick up cement blocks, car makers push car panels into place and astronauts assemble large parts on space stations. But when objects like cement blocks or car panels are heavy or we have to hold them out in front of us for a long time, our upper limbs can get tired. And the more tired we get, the harder it becomes to hold and move these objects the way we want to. Exoskeletons help by giving us a strong and solid frame for our upper limbs to rest inside. This frame can also give our shoulders, elbows, wrists and fingers extra strength. It can also help us push and pick up objects that are usually much too heavy for a human to move.

How You Can Help

As you can see, people with disabilities can get a lot of high-tech help. But what if you're not a scientist or robotics expert? How can you pitch in?

Treat Everyone with Respect

The first and most important way you can help is by treating people with disabilities the same as you would anyone else. Be friendly, respectful and willing to help if needed. Do not assume that a person with a disability either wants or requires assistance. Always ask first.

Support Organizations that Help

There are many organizations that help people with disabilities. In Canada, The War Amps uses its donations to provide prostheses to children. The Tetra Society of North America asks people to volunteer their time and expertise to build devices for people with disabilities. The device might be a cup that someone with physical difficulties can hold more easily or a tool they can use to grasp objects. Why not set up a lemonade stand with your friends or organize a fundraiser at school to support organizations like this in your area?

Get Technical

At school or in your spare time, explore mechanisms, electronics and computers—all are important in robotics and the design of technologies that people with disabilities can use. Even toys can help! Meccano or LEGO MINDSTORMS can be used to build working mechanisms and robots. And there are many YouTube videos that can help you, too. Just search "how to build an easy robot." You may not build a robotic prosthetic arm or exoskeleton on your first try, but you will learn a lot. And the more you learn, the more you'll be able to help. One day, you might even become a biomedical engineer and design robotics that people will be able to use.

A child with a below-knee prosthesis realizes her physical abilities and interest in sports while participating at the Milos Raonic Kids Agility Clinic held at Holland Bloorview Kids Rehabilitation Hospital.

Engineers test programmable
robot LEGO toys.

Glossary

3D printer
A printer that can make 3D objects from resin based on data inputted from a computer.

Artificial intelligence
The capability of a machine to imitate intelligent human behavior.

Assistive technology
Assistive, adaptive and rehabilitative devices for people with disabilities.

Cochlear implant
An advanced hearing aid that picks up sound from a microphone and sends signals to the inner ear through a bone behind the ear.

Exoskeleton
A rigid external covering for the body in some invertebrate animals, that provides both support and protection; a type of assistive robot that envelops the body to allow movement and strength.

Myoelectric sensor
A device that converts electric impulses in muscles to move prosthetic body parts.

Orthosis
An orthopedic appliance or apparatus used to support, align, prevent or correct deformities or to improve function of movable parts of the body.

Prosthesis
An artificial body part that is used to replace a broken or missing part of the body.

Robot
A machine capable of carrying out actions automatically, especially one programmable by a computer.

Wheelchair
A chair fitted with wheels for use as a means of transport by a person who is unable to walk as a result of illness, injury or disability.

Photo Credits

A technician adjusts a prosthetic foot.

Index